FIGHTING TO SURVIVE IN THE AMERICAN WEST
TERRIFYING TRUE STORIES

by Eric Braun

COMPASS POINT BOOKS
a capstone imprint

Fighting to Survive is published by
Compass Point Books, an imprint of Capstone.
1710 Roe Crest Drive, North Mankato, Minnesota 56003
www.capstonepub.com

**Library of Congress Cataloging-in-Publication Data is available
on the Library of Congress website**
ISBN: 978-0-7565-6431-5 (hardcover)
ISBN: 978-0-7565-6569-5 (paperback)
ISBN: 978-0-7565-6432-2 (ebook pdf)

Summary: Describes the terrifying true stories of people who survived extreme
weather, wild animal attacks, starvation, and other dangers in the American West.

Editorial Credits
Aaron J. Sautter, editor; Terri Poburka, designer; Morgan Walters, media researcher;
Kathy McColley, production specialist

Photo Credits
Alamy: Everett Collection Inc, 9, The History Collection, 41; Bridgeman Images:
Baraldi, Severino/Look and Learn, 11, 13, 14, The Hivernant, Wright, David H, 18;
Capstone Press, 27, 43, 50; Getty Images: Bettmann, 37, MPI, 20; Newscom: Danita
Delimont Photography, 8, Encyclopaedia Britannica/UIG Universal Images Group,
55, James Shaw/Photoshot, 19, Underwood Archives/UIG Universal Images Group,
5, Universal Images Group, 31; North Wind Picture Archives, 33, 34; Shutterstock:
Alexey Suloev, top Cover, Cynthia Liang, 53, diak, 42, Everett Historical, top 49,
bottom 49, Gary C. Tognoni, 47, Isaac Marzioli, design element throughout, James
Kirkikis, 38, Jim Pruitt, 16, Jiri Hrebicek, 24, KAMONRAT, (rock) Cover, kavram, 6,
Miloje, design element throughout, Philip Bird LRPS CPAGB, 23, RITTERFOTO, 45,
xpixel, design element throughout, Zack Frank, 57; Wikimedia: Andrew Parodi, 59

Printed and bound in the USA.
PA99

TABLE OF
CONTENTS

INTRODUCTION

The world today is small. Technology helps us get information about any place on Earth within seconds. We can see amazing photos of remote locations with a simple online search. We can video chat with people on the opposite side of the globe. And we can travel nearly anywhere we want with relative ease.

But the world wasn't always like it is today. Life was much more difficult in the days when people explored the frontier. It can be hard to imagine what life was like 200 years ago. The United States was still a young nation and most of its citizens lived close to the Atlantic Ocean. People gradually explored and settled in the West, but those bold men and women who first undertook those adventures had little idea what lay out there. The terrain was brutal. The weather was unforgiving. Food and water could be scarce. Freezing plains, towering mountains, walls of snow, deathly river rapids—brave explorers and pioneers faced all these challenges and more.

As the United States grew westward, white settlers and explorers also faced sometimes risky encounters with American Indian people. Unfortunately, white people had a long history of using lies, threats, and violence to force Indians off their land. Many Indians had good reason to distrust white people. Relations were peaceful with some Indian groups. But some groups were hostile toward whites. Regardless of the intentions of white settlers and explorers, the history of mistreatment by whites added danger to encounters with American Indians.

What drove people to explore the frontier? What made pioneers and explorers want to plunge into the unknown? Many wanted to find a new, better life for their families in the West, which was rumored to be sunny and mild and green. Some were tasked with opening up pathways that others could follow, making it easier for future generations. Some hardy souls just loved the adventure.

Whatever their motivation, they all needed to be well prepared and courageous. Danger and death lay in wait for them. Only the strong and the wise—and sometimes the lucky—would make it to their destinations alive.

A MOUNTAIN MAN'S MISSION
HUGH GLASS

One desire drove Hugh Glass more than anything else, perhaps even more than the basic instinct to survive. It was his wish for revenge. Miles from civilization, he had been mauled and severely injured by a bear. Two men were supposed to care for him until he recovered—or more likely until he died. Instead, they abandoned him, leaving him to suffer alone. In the end, his dogged pursuit of those men may be why he lived.

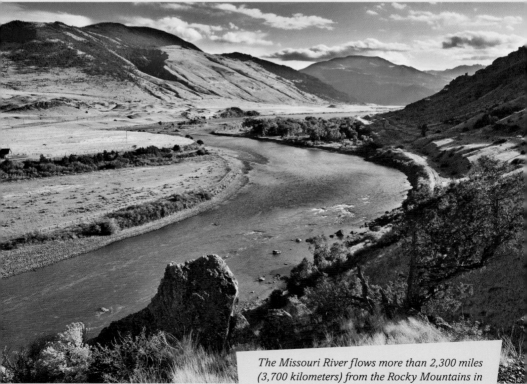

The Missouri River flows more than 2,300 miles (3,700 kilometers) from the Rocky Mountains in Montana until it joins the Mississippi River in St. Louis, Missouri.

Glass was one of the early fur trappers and adventurers known as mountain men. These tough men explored much of the American West during the first half of the 1800s. Many fascinating stories of mountain men have survived the years, but historical records are difficult to find. Some of the stories have been exaggerated or invented, and it's hard to be sure what is true. But historians have confirmed much of Glass's saga.

Glass was born probably around 1783 in the Philadelphia area. In his early career, he was a sailor. Though evidence is unclear, Glass may have been captured by the pirate Jean Lafitte around 1817. He was then forced into piracy until he escaped by swimming ashore near what is now Galveston, Texas. He began exploring and trapping furs in the West in the early 1820s.

By 1823 he was in St. Louis. That year he joined a group of 100 men organized by William Ashley, who was the lieutenant governor of Missouri and a militia general. The group's mission was to trap beaver on the Missouri River as they sailed 2,000 miles (3,220 kilometers) upriver to the recently established Fort Henry in what is now North Dakota. Working against the river's current, the journey was slow and difficult.

TRADING AND CONFLICT

Continuing north, the group stopped to trade with the Arikara nation. These American Indians had a fenced village along the river. The Arikara had recently had conflicts with other fur-trapping companies over fair payments for their furs. The conflicts had led to violence, and several Arikara warriors had been killed. Ashley's company hadn't been involved in those battles. But the Arikara still wanted payment for the deaths of their men. Ashley gave them gifts, which the Arikara seemed to accept. The white men traded rifles and ammunition for horses. From the Arikara village, Ashley planned to send half his crew over land with the horses and supplies to Fort Henry. The rest of the men would continue to take the boats upriver.

Though the trading appeared to be peaceful, there was trouble later that night when two of Ashley's men went into the village. A fight broke out and one of them was killed. The Arikara then attacked the main company at dawn. After a short battle, several men were killed on both sides. Hugh Glass was shot in the leg.

Arikara Indians usually lived in earth lodges built next to rivers on the Great Plains. The villages later became centers of trade during the mid-1800s.

Ashley's fur trappers retreated downriver to recover and prepare for their next move. Ashley sent for Andrew Henry, an experienced frontiersman who was stationed at Fort Henry. Henry came from the fort with more horses. The men decided to abandon the idea of traveling the river. Hugh Glass was part of the first band of men who left with Henry to travel overland to the fort. A second group waited while more horses were acquired.

DID YOU KNOW?

Another famous mountain man led the second group of Ashley's men. Jedediah Smith had a reputation as a courageous fighter and explorer. Like Glass, Smith was attacked by a large grizzly bear during the fall of 1823. The bear knocked Smith to the ground, breaking his ribs and tearing open his side. The bear even took Smith's head in its mouth. After the bear left him, other men in Smith's party rushed to his side. His scalp and ear had been torn off and lay on the ground. Smith coached a friend to sew them back onto his head. For the rest of his life, he wore his hair long to cover the wicked scar.

GRIZZLY ATTACK

Glass, Henry, and about 30 men left the river in August 1823. The group had made it to the upper Grand River in South Dakota when Glass heard a terrifying roar.

As one of the group's hunters, Glass was walking ahead of the others with his rifle. He scanned the brush along the river bottom, looking for game. When he heard an animal's roar, he looked up to see a grizzly bear charging at him. He had just enough time to notice two bear cubs nearby. That was bad news. It meant the grizzly was a mother bear. Protecting her young was a job she took very seriously.

Glass barely had time to raise his rifle and get off a shot. But it didn't stop the angry bear. With massive paws and razor-sharp claws, she shredded his back and arms. Hearing his cries for help, the rest of the men ran to catch up. They shot and killed the bear. By then, however, Glass's throat was slashed, and chunks of flesh were ripped from his back.

Henry and the rest of the men assumed Glass would die overnight. But in the morning, he was still alive. The men were in dangerous territory, where they were vulnerable to Indian attacks. Glass's injury put everyone in danger. It was risky to stay where they were. Henry decided the men would have to carry Glass.

The men built a stretcher and walked with Glass for two days. But carrying the injured man slowed them considerably. The group was still in danger of attack. So Henry paid two men a bonus to stay with Glass until he died and give him a proper burial. The rest of the group would go on ahead to the fort.

Glass slashed the bear several times with his knife, but he was no match for the powerful animal.

WAITING FOR DEATH

One of the men who took the offer was an experienced mountain man named John Fitzgerald. The other was Jim Bridger, a young man who was on his first adventure west. The two expected Glass to die quickly, but after five days he was still hanging on. He wasn't moving. He wasn't talking. But he kept breathing.

The longer the men waited with Glass, the more worried they became. What if they were attacked? What if they fell so far behind that they couldn't catch up to the others?

Eventually Fitzgerald convinced Bridger that it was OK to leave Glass alone. Surely the crumpled, bloody man would die at any moment. They had already stayed longer than anyone had expected. They moved Glass to a spot by a spring, took his rifle, knife, and fire-making kit—none of which a dead man would need—and left for Fort Henry.

RECOVERY

But Hugh Glass wasn't a dead man yet. Instead, he somehow began to regain strength. Soon he realized that he had been abandoned, and he crawled back toward the river. He knew there was a trading post on the river where he could recover. He could also get supplies there for his next task—to find the men who had abandoned him and kill them.

At first his only food came from eating berries, roots, and insects. Some stories say that he later found a bison that had been killed by wolves. He ate after the wolves had their fill. The meat helped him regain his strength. When he reached the Missouri River, he got a boat from Lakota Indians and floated to the trading post at Fort Kiowa in present-day South Dakota. It was mid-October 1823. He had traveled about 250 miles (402 km) since being left for dead. But it was only the beginning of his long journey toward revenge.

Fearing another Indian attack, John Fitzgerald and Jim Bridger took Glass's weapons and left him to die alone in the wild.

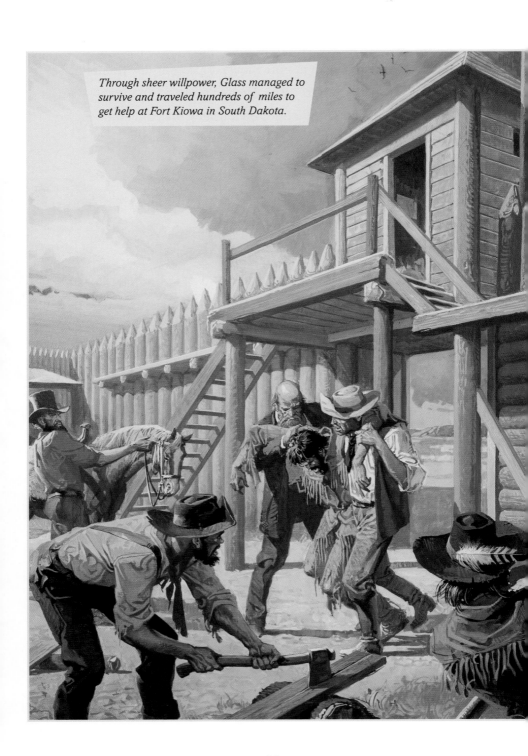

Through sheer willpower, Glass managed to survive and traveled hundreds of miles to get help at Fort Kiowa in South Dakota.

ANOTHER CLOSE CALL

Within a few days, Glass heard about a party of men who were heading 300 miles (483 km) upriver to trade with the Mandan Indians. The Mandan lived in a village near Fort Henry, where Glass believed Fitzgerald and Bridger were. Glass was still recovering from his injuries and long journey. But he was determined to find the men who had abandoned him. He borrowed money to buy a rifle, ammunition, and other supplies, and joined the expedition.

Glass and the five other men rowed upstream for six weeks before they neared the Mandan village. The village was on the other side of a U-shaped bend in the river, called an oxbow. When they came to the oxbow, Glass got off the boat and traveled by foot to the village. He thought it would be faster than rowing around the oxbow, and he was eager to find Fitzgerald and Bridger as quickly as possible. It was a fortunate decision, because the Arikara ambushed the men in the boat. All five were killed.

But Glass wasn't safe yet. As he walked toward the Mandan village, some Arikara spotted him and sent warriors to kill him. But the Mandan also saw Glass, and they were closer. They sent two men to grab Glass before he was killed. The Mandan took Glass to a nearby trading post run by the Columbia Fur Company.

This incident marked Glass's third close call with the Arikara. But that fact didn't seem to affect him. He was determined to continue and left the trading post after dark that night. It was now late November, and cold winter weather was closing in.

MEETING BRIDGER

Glass walked for 38 days across the cold, windy land. When he finally arrived at Fort Henry, however, he found it empty. Weeks earlier, frustrated by not trapping many furs in this location, Andrew Henry had established a new Fort Henry about 30 miles (48 km) away. Historians aren't sure how Glass knew where to go. There may have been a note at the old fort. However he figured it out, Glass set out for the new Fort Henry.

At last, after having walked hundreds of miles across the deadly cold Dakota Territories, he arrived at the fort on December 31, 1823. The men there were shocked to see him. After all, they thought he'd died and been buried. Glass assured them he wasn't a ghost, and that he was very much alive. And he wanted to see Jim Bridger and John Fitzgerald.

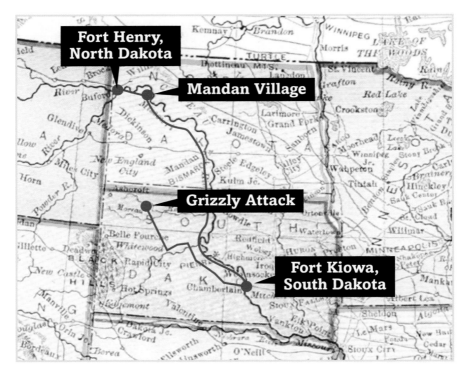

Fort Henry, North Dakota

Mandan Village

Grizzly Attack

Fort Kiowa, South Dakota

Unfortunately for Glass, Fitzgerald was no longer at the fort. Though Glass was extremely disappointed, he did get to confront Bridger. But after talking with the young man, he realized that Fitzgerald was the one who was responsible for leaving Glass to die alone. The older man had pressured Bridger to go along with his decision. Glass decided to forgive Bridger.

Glass learned that Fitzgerald was probably on his way to Fort Atkinson, a military fort near present-day Omaha, Nebraska. But the winter weather had turned severe, and Glass had to wait before pursuing him. He finally got his chance on February 29, 1824. Henry sent Glass and four other men to Fort Atkinson to deliver an update to General Ashley.

The men traveled along the North Platte River until the ice thawed, at which time they built boats and floated down the river. Along the way they were attacked once again by Arikara Indians who were camped along the river. Two of the men were killed, and Glass and the other two scattered. As he had before, Glass found himself traveling by foot hundreds of miles from the fort without a rifle, which he'd lost when he fled.

He didn't totally despair, though. He later told a fellow trapper, "Although I had lost my rifle and all my plunder, I felt quite rich when I found my knife, flint and steel in my shot pouch. These little fixens make a man feel right peart when he is three or four hundred miles from anybody or any place."

FINAL DISAPPOINTMENT

Glass assumed more Arikara were camped along the river, so he left the river and headed by land toward Fort Kiowa, which was several hundred miles away. It was the same fort he traveled to after the grizzly attack. It was buffalo calving season, and Glass was able to kill and eat several calves as he traveled. Due in part to the abundant meat, he arrived at Fort Kiowa in good health. There he learned that Fitzgerald had enlisted in the army and was definitely at Fort Atkinson. Loaded with fresh supplies, Glass headed toward that fort.

Hugh Glass was one of several mountain men that worked for William Ashley. These tough men relied on their experience and survival skills while hunting and trapping for furs in the rugged wilderness.

In June 1824, Glass arrived at Fort Atkinson. Believing revenge was at last within reach, he demanded to see Fitzgerald. But Fitzgerald was a U.S. soldier now—government property—and the army captain on duty refused to let Glass see him. He likely didn't want a U.S. soldier to be killed. After listening to Glass's story, however, he did retrieve the mountain man's rifle from Fitzgerald and returned it to Glass.

Glass had been nearly killed by a bear and left for dead. He had been involved in four Indian attacks in which dozens of men had been killed. And he had traveled hundreds of miles—mostly by foot. After all that, he wasn't going to get his final revenge. But he was thrilled to have his trusted firearm again. That would have to satisfy him.

DID YOU KNOW?
The 2015 film *The Revenant* was loosely based on Hugh Glass's incredible story of survival. Glass was played by actor Leonardo DiCaprio. He won several Best Actor awards for his performance as the tough mountain man.

ROCKY MOUNTAIN CASTAWAY
JANETTE RIKER

Life on the frontier was hard and dangerous for the brave souls who lived and traded there. They faced threats from wild animals. They had to hunt for their food. They had to shelter themselves from the harsh elements, often in temperatures that plummeted far below zero. But the hardy pioneers were strong and experienced. Most of the time they had friends, family, or other explorers to help with the work and provide some company.

Settlers carried everything they owned in covered wagons as they traveled west on the Oregon Trail.

However, when Janette Riker found herself facing winter in the mountains, she had none of those benefits. Her family had disappeared. She had no gun to hunt for food or defend herself. And she was only 14 years old.

By the mid-1840s, many Americans were heading west along the Oregon Trail to claim open land on the frontier. Janette, whose mother had died earlier, set out for Oregon with her father and two brothers early in 1849. They were just four out of about 30,000 people who migrated west that year.

By late September, the Rikers had reached the mountains in present-day Montana. They made camp in a green valley, where

they could rest their oxen and hunt for meat to restock their supplies. After the short break, they planned to head up into the high mountains on their way to the other side.

On the first morning, Janette's father and brothers took their rifles and went off to hunt buffalo. Janette may have watched them as their figures grew smaller in the distance and finally disappeared. It was the last time she would ever see them.

ALONE ON THE EDGE OF WINTER

When the men didn't return that night, Janette slept in the wagon. She must have been quite frightened, and not only because her family hadn't returned. The howls of wolves filled the valley outside the wagon. How would she defend herself if the beasts attacked?

Early the next morning, Janette got up and followed the trail her father and brothers had taken. She hiked for miles into a deep gorge. She was able to follow their tracks at first. But soon she lost them, and she returned to camp. The next day she searched again. She called their names and hiked farther. She searched every day for a week until she realized that they weren't coming back. Whatever happened to her now, she would have to face it alone.

Janette sized up her situation. It was clear that the snow line in the mountains was getting lower and would reach her camp soon. She knew that she wouldn't be able to travel over the mountains alone. Her only choice was to make a camp that would last through the winter.

The tools in the wagon included axes and shovels. With these, Janette built a hut by lashing together poles and small logs. To keep out the wind and snow, she stuffed dried grass into the gaps between logs and piled dirt around the sides of the structure. She then pulled off the wagon canvas, stretched it over the shelter, and staked it to the ground. Her hut was sealed from rain and snowfall and would protect her from the wind. Finally, she brought the stove

from the wagon into the hut to keep it warm. At the top of her shelter, she made a hole for the smoke to escape. Then she set to work cutting as much firewood as possible for fuel to burn all winter.

All this time, the oxen had been feeding on sweet grass and getting fatter. Janette slaughtered the fattest one and butchered it. After cutting up the meat, she salted it and stored it away for the winter.

Janette Riker made her camp in a valley in western Montana that provided firewood and water to last through the winter.

SURVIVING DAY BY DAY

By November the snow began to fall hard, blanketing the valley. Janette spent most of her time inside her warm shelter, huddled beneath blankets. She kept her store of firewood nearby, so it was easy to fetch when she needed it. As the days grew shorter and colder, the snow nearly buried her hut, forcing Janette to dig out her smoke hole. At night, a mountain lion and wolves prowled outside her hut, attracted by the smell of the oxen meat.

However, Janette and the meat stayed safe inside the sturdy hut for the entire winter. The daily tasks of getting wood, stoking the fire, and preparing food likely helped to distract her. But she no doubt thought about her missing family often. She must have assumed they were dead. The loneliness would have been a burden just as heavy as the hard work of survival.

During the long winter, hungry wolves and mountain lions threatened Janette's small shelter and food supply.

Eventually spring brought warmer weather, which meant melting snow. This created a new challenge for Janette, as the water flowed through the valley—and right through her shelter. She quickly began moving her belongings out of the hut and back into the wagon. She had to lug her heavy, waterlogged blankets and other supplies across the soaked, muddy ground. But she managed to move everything, including the stove and the canvas, which she reattached to the wagon.

SAVED IN SPRING

Janette was safe inside the wagon, but everything was soaked, including her firewood. For two weeks she was unable to make a fire. She was warm enough, but she couldn't cook the meat. So she ate it raw with uncooked cornmeal instead. The unhealthy diet and wet conditions began to weaken her.

Finally, in late April, an Indian hunting party found Janette. By this time, she was desperately weak. But the Indians were impressed by Janette's toughness and how she survived the winter alone. They fed her and helped her regain her strength. Then they carried her and some of her goods to a white settlement at Walla Walla in Washington.

Not much is known about Janette's life after her incredible Montana winter. It's known that she later married. As for her brothers and father, history is silent on what happened to them. It's thought that they simply got lost or fell into a gorge. Their family name, however, lived on in Janette Riker, courageous pioneer.

SNOWED IN WITH DEATH
THE DONNER PARTY

Like any parents, George and Tamsen Donner wanted to provide a better life for their family. Lush farmland and fortune lay out in California. So the Donners, like thousands of others in the years before the Civil War, headed west. Unfortunately, their journey was doomed to become one of the darkest stories in American history.

Tamsen had been married before, but her husband and two young children died of disease. After moving to Illinois, she met and married George Donner. George had been married twice before, but both his wives had died. He had two daughters, Elitha and Leanna. He and Tamsen had three more daughters together, Frances, Georgia, and Eliza. When the family left on their journey, 14-year-old Elitha was the oldest. The youngest, Eliza, was just three.

The Donner family left Springfield, Illinois, on April 14 or 15, 1846. George's brother, Jacob, and his family joined them. James F. Reed and his family joined them as well. The party totaled 31 people spread out over nine wagons.

On May 10, the families arrived at Independence, Missouri, at the beginning of the Oregon Trail. After setting out from Independence, they joined another group of about 50 wagons. The groups traveled together for several weeks until they reached Fort Laramie, Wyoming. It was here that a fateful decision would be made.

THE HASTINGS CUTOFF

A man named Lansford W. Hastings had created a different trail to California, one that was separate from the established Oregon Trail. He sent letters to many travelers on the Oregon Trail telling them that his trail was faster and safer. The large group left Fort Laramie together until they came to the Little Sandy River. There they could choose to follow the established trail or head for Fort Bridger and then take the "Hastings Cutoff." Most of the group stuck to the main trail.

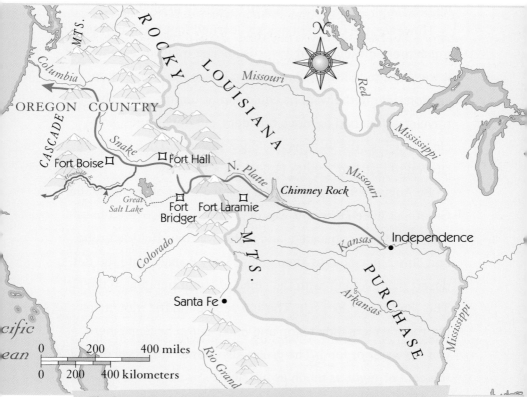

The Oregon Trail stretched 2,130 miles (3,428 km) across western prairies and mountains from Independence, Missouri, to Oregon City, Oregon.

The group that decided to head to Fort Bridger included the two Donner families and the Reed family. They elected George Donner as their leader. When they arrived at Fort Bridger, Hastings was no longer there, but Jim Bridger was. At this point, the Donner party could have turned north and rejoined the Oregon Trail. But Bridger convinced them that the Hastings Cutoff would be quicker. He also told them that it was smooth, safe, and had plenty of water. Unfortunately, none of this would prove to be true.

After resting for four days and restocking supplies, the Donner Party left Fort Bridger on the Hastings Cutoff on July 31. More people had decided to join the group, which increased the size of the party to nearly 90 people.

However, the travelers quickly learned that the trail was much more difficult than advertised. The trail was so new that it was hard to follow in some areas. It also ran along steep canyons where the wagons could slip or tumble over. The travelers often had to move boulders, cut down trees, and clear brush so the wagons could get through. Their progress slowed to just 1 to 2 miles (1.6 to 3.2 km) a day.

By August 29 they reached a valley. Ahead of them lay the Great Salt Lake Desert. It was dry, barren, and covered in salt. The oxen were exhausted, and water was low. But the group had little choice but to keep going. They walked onto the flat desert that evening, with the smell of sulfur hanging in the air. The wind tasted like salt. The sun set behind the mountains, but the travelers didn't stop and make camp because there was no water or food. The group also wanted to travel during the cool of night as much as possible.

The salty desert glowed under the light of the moon. Dry salt crackled underfoot. In damp areas, the salt gummed up and caused the wagon wheels to sink. Late at night, the temperatures were bone-chilling. At dawn, the settlers' shadows grew out in front of them. Several members of the party grew dehydrated and began to hallucinate. They thought they saw lakes or other wagons. Some of the oxen broke free of the wagons and ran, driven insane with thirst.

Finally, on September 26, the party rejoined the traditional trail at the Humboldt River. They had set off on the Hastings Cutoff two months before and had lost a month of travel time. This was a critical loss because the hardest part of the journey was yet to come—the Sierra Nevada Mountains. The lost month meant that the Donner Party had little time before winter set in. If snow came early, they would be in real trouble.

DID YOU KNOW?

Jim Bridger had a long career as a mountain man, fur trapper, explorer, and guide for travelers in the West. As a young man he was part of Hugh Glass's expedition into the wilderness. Bridger later became one of the first explorers to see the geysers at Yellowstone National Park and the Great Salt Lake in Utah. Later in life, Bridger discovered Bridger Pass, which helped to shorten the length of the Oregon Trail. He also established the Bridger Trail that led from Wyoming to Montana.

DEADLY FIGHT IN THE DESERT

By this time many in the group were arguing. James Reed, who had pushed hard to take the Hastings Cutoff, was blamed for the disastrous decision. Tempers came to a head on October 5 when the group prepared to climb a pass. One of the hired men, John Snyder, got his team of oxen tangled with another man's team. An argument started, and James Reed got involved. Snyder threatened Reed with a whip, and as Reed's wife Margaret tried to break up the fight, she was struck on the head. Reed pulled a knife and stabbed Snyder in the chest. Snyder fell into another man's arms. The man helped Snyder to the ground, where he died.

The Donner Party had a meeting that night about what to do. Some wanted to hang Reed right then and there. But instead, they decided to banish him from the party. Reed attended the funeral for Snyder and then headed west on his horse alone.

The rest of the party continued walking across the desert, mostly by night, until October 17. It was not yet dawn as the party began climbing a steep, sandy hill. Later that morning, they reached a glorious sight. The Truckee River ran cold, quick, and clear out of the mountains. Each of the travelers knelt on the bank and drank deeply.

After a short rest, the pioneers began the journey across the Sierra Nevada mountains in hopes of beating the snow. On the other side was their goal, California. They crisscrossed the Truckee River as they traveled up the pass, avoiding boulders and looking for an easy passage. High above them, dark clouds surrounded the mountain peaks as the settlers headed into a thick pine forest.

With snow beginning to fly, the group camped in a grassy meadow on October 30. The next morning, they woke up to a few inches of snow on the ground. They packed up and continued their trek, sloshing through the snow. Many of the settlers' shoes had worn through, and the cold snow was painful on their feet. That afternoon, they walked out of the woods near the south end of Truckee Lake, which is called Donner Lake today.

Up ahead stood tall rock cliffs rising more than 1,100 feet (335 meters) above the water. A notch ran through the cliffs. That notch was supposed to be their path, but it was quickly filling with snow.

Donner Lake lies near the mountain pass where the Donner Party attempted to cross over to reach California.

STUCK AT THE PASS

Some families attempted to get through the pass, but the snow was up to the axles on the wagons. As they climbed higher, the deep snow was 3 to 4 feet (0.9 to 1.2 m) high. In some spots, the wind had blown the snow into 10-foot (3-m) drifts. The oxen and mules fell as they trudged through the snow, and the iron-rimmed wagon wheels slid on the ice. After several days, another storm rolled in. Several women, who were carrying the children, lay down in the snow, exhausted. Some men lit a tree on fire for warmth. Everyone bundled up and fell asleep. When they woke up the next morning, they and the field where they lay were covered in more snow.

The families had to retreat and find shelter. One family found an old shack, which an earlier settler had built after becoming snowbound in the same spot. The group built two more cabins, and all 59 people huddled in the shanties to wait.

Meanwhile, the Donner families were dealing with their own struggles. One of their wagons had flipped over earlier. Young Eliza and Georgia were temporarily trapped inside the wagon. The girls were unhurt, but one of the wagon's axles had broken in the fall. While George and Jacob made a new axle, George gashed his hand with a chisel. It wasn't a bad wound, but it quickly became infected. Dealing with the accident had caused the Donners to fall behind the main group.

When the Donner families caught up to the others, they realized it would be impossible to cross the pass. They began to build a cabin, but Jacob was in poor health. Between that and George's bad hand, they couldn't work very fast. Even 14-year-old Elitha helped out by notching logs. But the snow was falling too fast. They had to hastily construct tents out of quilts, buffalo robes, and brush.

The snow fell for eight more days. The struggling settlers had little luck hunting animals. With supplies running low, they had to slaughter their remaining cattle for food. They made use of every part of the animals, salting and stacking meat to preserve it. Even so, it wasn't long before meat was scarce. People ate animal hides. They ate oxen hide rugs. They boiled bones to make soup. They boiled the bones so many times that they became soft enough to eat.

Growing desperate, some people tried to cross the pass on foot, but they had to turn back. Meanwhile, James Reed, the banished murderer, had reached California and was trying to get back to the party with supplies. He had horses, a mule, beef, and flour. But he was unable to get across the pass to bring it to them.

Heavy snow made it impossible for the settlers to travel through the narrow mountain pass.

A GRISLY DECISION

Desperate hunger began to seep in among the group. Two men died of malnutrition. In early December, some of the settlers made snowshoes by weaving strips of oxen hide across the U-shaped oxbows. On December 16, a group of 17 set out with the snowshoes to try to get across the pass. They hiked for days, making slow progress in the deep snow. They were already weak and malnourished, and none of them had experience camping in such extreme conditions. Around December 25, they were caught in a severe blizzard. They circled up and held their blankets overhead to preserve the group's body heat and keep off the snow.

This action kept them warm enough, but the tiny, cramped space was filthy and smelly. Patrick Dolan became delirious with hypothermia and died. Soon after, members of the snowshoe party

While stuck in the mountain pass, the settlers could do little more than huddle together and try to stay warm in the harsh winter weather.

made a grisly decision. To avoid starving to death, they ate the flesh from Dolan's body. Three others died around the same time, and the remaining members of the party ate them too. They divided the meat so that nobody would have to eat someone from their own family.

On January 17 the surviving members of the snowshoe group finally had a glimmer of hope. After 33 days since leaving Truckee Lake, the group arrived at a ranch at the edge of the Sacramento Valley.

FIRST RESCUE PARTY

Mostly women and children were left behind at the Truckee Lake camp. Most of the men had gone on the snowshoe expedition to improve their chances of finding help. One day Tamsen Donner took 3-year-old Eliza to another shelter to play with her cousins. But the sight of the hollow faces of the others scared the little girl, and she was glad return to her own shelter. Surely things and people were just as dreary there, but at least she was used to them.

When a blizzard hit the camp, the pioneers huddled in their shelters and listened to the howling wind. Starvation, exhaustion, and cold led to the death of several people, including babies and children. The Reed family grew so hungry that they ate their dog. "We ate his head and feet and hide and every thing about him," one of the children later wrote.

On February 18 seven rescuers arrived at the Truckee Lake cabins. James Reed and the survivors of the snowshoe party had alerted citizens in San Francisco to the settlers' dreadful situation in the mountains. When the rescuers began to call out, the trapped settlers were stunned. One woman, Levinah Murphy, climbed up the snow-carved steps from a cabin and stared at the rescuers. "Are you men from California or do you come from heaven?" she asked.

HARD DECISIONS

The rescuers were taken aback by the camp's conditions. Dead bodies were buried in the snow. The survivors were extremely thin and weak, and many couldn't stand. The smell inside the cabins was overwhelming. The rescue party shared dried meat and biscuits. Then they went on to the camp where the Donner family was. Conditions there were even worse. George's arm was full of gangrene. The children could barely walk.

The rescue party discussed with George Donner who would go back on the first return trip. They didn't have enough supplies or men to take everyone. They also had to hurry. Another blizzard could hit at any time. It was a difficult discussion. Those who stayed behind might die.

Because of his injury, George Donner was too weak to make the journey. Tamsen refused to leave him behind, so she stayed as well. George and Tamsen decided Elitha and Leanna would leave with the rescue party. The rescuers cut fresh firewood for those staying behind and rationed out the tiny bit of food that they could spare. Tamsen tied blankets around Elitha and Leanna and watched the party leave again. She must have felt deep sadness. She and the others had hoped for months that someone would rescue them. When someone finally came, she had to send off part of her family while staying behind to face the possibility of death.

After the rescue crew was gone, those remaining at the camps discussed a terrible but unavoidable conclusion. Buried in the snow was the meat they needed to survive. There is no record of who was the

first to act. But eventually they all agreed. If they were to live, they would have to eat the dead.

At the Donner cabin, the first body they found was that of Jacob Donner, who had died in December. They asked permission from his wife, Elizabeth, who agreed. George and Tamsen fed their daughters with meat from George's brother, but George couldn't even watch, let alone join them.

Rescuers made a gruesome discovery when they arrived at the camp in February 1847. The settlers had survived by eating the flesh of the dead.

FINAL RESCUES AND SALVAGE

A second rescue party arrived at the camp on March 1. James Reed was with them, and he was reunited with his children. This group took 14 children and three adults back across the mountains to California. Once again, Tamsen stayed behind with her husband. Reed promised her that another rescue unit was due soon, so she kept her three remaining daughters with her as well.

A monument in Truckee, California, honors the memory of the Donner Party and those who lost their lives in search of a new life in the West.

VIRILE TO RISK AND FIND; KINDLY WITHAL AND A READY HELP. FACING THE BRUNT OF FATE; INDOMITABLE,—UNAFRAID.

The third relief party arrived at the Truckee camps on March 12. Once again, Tamsen chose to stay with her husband, George, even though she was told that no other rescue parties were coming. George couldn't travel, and she wouldn't leave him alone. She did, however, send her daughters out with this final rescue party.

On April 17 a salvage party arrived at the site to collect any possessions that were left behind and rescue any surviving adults. The only living person they found was Louis Keseberg. George and Tamsen Donner had died several days before the party arrived. Keseberg had been alone for days, perhaps weeks, surrounded by dead bodies. But he was too weak to properly dispose of the remains.

The Donner Party's journey west, which had begun more than a year before, was finally over. Of all the people trapped in the mountain camps, only 45 survived. George and Tamsen, who wanted to provide a better life for their children, had been among the last to die. Their daughters, however, all lived long and prosperous lives.

DID YOU KNOW?

The third relief group included two men, William Eddy and William Foster, who had left as part of the snowshoe party months earlier. They were eager to save their sons, who had stayed behind. But when they arrived at the camps, they found that both their sons had died. Not only that, but another man, Louis Keseberg, was accused of eating part of Eddy's son. Eddy vowed to murder him if he ever made it to California.

NEAR REBELLION ABOVE YOSEMITE
JOSEPH WALKER

Joseph Walker looked over his men. They were ragged, cold, hungry, frustrated—and desperate. Who could blame them? It was October 18, 1833, and they had been traveling since late July, when they left Fort Bonneville in Wyoming. Now they were camping in the snow high in the Sierra Nevada Mountains. They were living with reduced rations and often had no fire due to the wet conditions. At night they shivered as they slept in wet clothes, fearful of avalanches and falling boulders. During the day they blazed their own trail, hacking their way forward at an agonizingly slow pace.

The men respected Walker, who was a well-known explorer. But he knew that if he didn't do something, they would abandon him and turn back. There wasn't enough food to last until they got back to plentiful hunting grounds. The smart choice was to keep going. But the men were afraid. As he looked at them now, their breath coming out in hard, white puffs, he understood. They were ready to take desperate action. Walker was facing a rebellion.

Joseph Walker came from a long line of explorers and adventurers. His family lived in eastern Tennessee when he was born in 1798. Like the other men in his family, he was tall and strong. He was also intelligent and clever. One of Walker's earliest adventures as a mountain man came at age 22, when he joined an illegal hunting and trapping expedition into what is now New Mexico. He was imprisoned for a short time in Santa Fe by the Spanish military. Ironically, he later served as the sheriff of Jackson County, Missouri. After two terms as sheriff, he traded horses at military posts.

In 1830 Walker met Benjamin Bonneville, a U.S. army captain and another great explorer. Bonneville offered Walker a position in 1833 as a field commander on a trapping and trading expedition into the West. His goal was to find a path across the Sierra Nevada Mountains into California. Walker's experience made him a great choice. He had been trapping since he was a boy. He had taken multiple trips into the Rocky Mountains, including one to Santa Fe.

He had moved large numbers of horses and other animals over long distances. Walker also had an excellent reputation from his time as a sheriff. He was knowledgeable and levelheaded. Walker gladly accepted Bonneville's offer. He was eager for the chance to explore farther into the frontier.

Joseph Walker in 1860

A WELL-STOCKED PARTY

Walker left Fort Bonneville on July 27, 1833, with 58 men and more than 200 horses loaded with supplies intended to last at least a year. They carried blankets, bison robes, beaver traps, ropes, firearms, ammunition, kettles, and horseshoes. Each man carried 60 pounds of bison jerky, which they planned to replenish through hunting animals along the way.

One man in the party, Zenas Leonard, was an experienced mountain man who kept a detailed diary of the trip. Before the trip, Leonard wrote, "Mr. Walker was a man well calculated to undertake a business of this kind. He was well hardened to the hardships of the wilderness . . . was kind and affable to his men, but at the same time at liberty to command without giving offence—and to explore unknown regions was his chief delight."

Walker's group scouted around Utah's Great Salt Lake in August. They later camped with a hunting party of Bannocks, a group of American Indians who gave Walker information about the area. Based on this, he chose a path directly west from the lake through the desert.

Around September 1, the group made it to the Humboldt River. They followed it downstream across what is today the state of Nevada. They camped near a lake when they got their first look at the big mountain range that lay ahead of them. According to Leonard's diary, they set out "in the direction of a mountain, which was in sight, and which we could see was covered with snow on its summit." When they had climbed high enough up the mountain, they could see the plains of Nevada to the east. Leonard wrote that they were "awfully sublime."

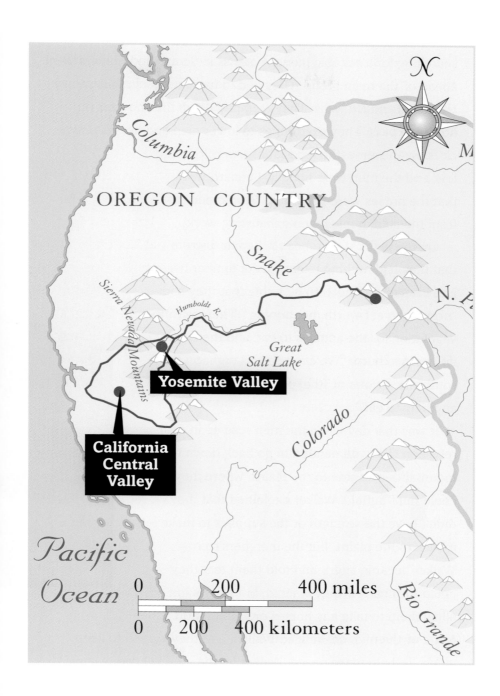

NOTHING TO EAT WORTH MENTIONING

For a month the men worked their way up the mountain, searching for a suitable passage across it. Scouts and hunters went ahead of the main group. They had to navigate dangerous snowy crevasses and icy walls. They stomped down the snow for the horses to pass. They used ropes to lower men and horses down cliffs. By this time, the food rations were running low, and the men were hungry. Leonard wrote that the horses were becoming "stupid and stiff" from the cold, hunger, and exhausting work.

On the night of October 17, Leonard wrote that they had nothing to eat except juniper berries and insects. On the 18th he wrote that they had "nothing to eat worth mentioning." There was no vegetation for the animals to eat, and there was no wood to burn. "We camped this night on the south side of one of [the] peaks or ridges without anything to eat."

It was that day when the men rose up in near rebellion. They demanded to go back down the mountain's east side to the plains, where they could hunt buffalo. Walker explained that they didn't have the strength or the supplies to make it back to the plains, but the men persisted. Walker became angry and told them that they could turn back if they wanted, but he wouldn't allow them to take any horses or ammunition. None of the men challenged Walker, and they agreed to keep going. To help make peace, Walker let the men kill two of their horses for food.

Leonard wrote, "This gave our men fresh courage, and we went to bed this night in better spirits than we had done for a long time." He added that many of the men ate "as eagerly of this black, tough, lean, horse flesh, as if it had been the choicest piece of beef steak."

The rocky terrain in the Sierra Nevada mountains offered no shelter and little food for the men and horses in Walker's party.

REACHING YOSEMITE

But the explorers' troubles weren't over. When they reached the main ridge, it took several more days to find a safe path down to the west. Finally, they came upon a magnificent view—the Yosemite Valley. Its massive waterfalls and mighty redwood trees were a natural spectacle that none of the men had ever seen. In fact, they were perhaps the first white people ever to see it.

However, Leonard wrote that they didn't take much time to admire the beautiful scene. Rather, they continued to look for a safe way down the mountain. The going was slow, and the men were getting discouraged again. But then one day they came to an outlook where they could see the plains and valley below—the Central Valley of California. Walker assured the men that they were sure to make it now, and they trusted him. As Leonard wrote, Walker "was a man well acquainted with geography."

The next day the travelers discovered a trail going down the ridge. After following it for a while, they spotted and killed a deer—the largest game they had taken in weeks. They stopped and cooked it on the spot, eating it quickly.

From that point on, as they made their way down the mountain and the snow became shallower, the men's spirits were bright. The hunting became more plentiful, and at night they sat around the campfire and talked about the beauty they had witnessed.

Walker's party spent the winter in California and returned east the following spring. Later in their lives, the men recalled the journey across the Sierras as a great one. And the day they first witnessed the Yosemite Valley was among the greatest moments of their lives.

Yosemite Valley at Yosemite National Park, California

DID YOU KNOW?

Today, Yosemite is one of the most popular National Parks in the United States. It is famous for its beautiful natural waterfalls, deep valleys, and giant sequoia trees. It attracts about 4 million visitors each year.

INTO THE UNKNOWN
LEWIS AND CLARK

By the dawn of the 1800s, the United States and its territories extended from the Atlantic Ocean east to the Mississippi River. The nation was only about 25 years old, but President Thomas Jefferson and other politicians assumed it would continue to grow over the years. For this to happen, it was critical for the United States to have the ability to use the Mississippi and the port of New Orleans for shipping goods.

In 1803 when negotiating to secure those rights, the opportunity came to purchase the entire Louisiana Territory. The Louisiana Territory was a huge area of land—about 828,000 square miles (2.1 million square km)—west of the Mississippi. At that time France controlled the territory. U.S. negotiators bought it for $15 million. The purchase more than doubled the size of the United States.

President Jefferson was eager to explore America's new land. He appointed Meriwether Lewis, an army captain and Jefferson's personal secretary, to lead an expedition. Lewis chose army lieutenant William Clark to accompany him.

Jefferson's goals for the mission included finding the best ways to travel across the continent to enable trade with other nations. He also wanted to learn what resources the newly acquired land would provide. And perhaps most importantly, he wanted to make it clear to the native peoples that the United States now owned this vast area of land.

Meriwether Lewis

William Clark

Lewis and Clark knew that exploring the Louisiana Territory would be a huge job. They had little knowledge of the land to the west. They began collecting supplies and recruiting men to be a part of their "Corps of Volunteers for Northwest Discovery." The group of 43—plus a dog named Seaman—left Camp Dubois in Illinois on May 14, 1804, heading upstream on the Missouri River.

SACAGAWEA JOINS THE PARTY

The expedition team met several Indian tribes along the way. Most of them were peaceful. Lewis and Clark presented them with gifts and traded goods. They also informed the Indians that the United States now owned the land, and that the country wanted to peacefully trade goods with them. In early November, the team stopped near present-day Washburn, North Dakota, to camp for the winter. They built a fort there, Fort Mandan, and spent the winter hunting and making supplies such as canoes and clothing.

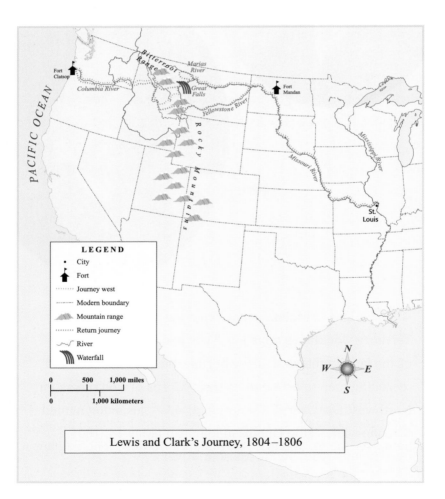

Lewis and Clark's Journey, 1804–1806

That winter they also met a French-Canadian trapper named Toussaint Charbonneau, whom they hired as an interpreter. Charbonneau's Shoshone wife, 16-year-old Sacagawea, would join them to help communicate with any Shoshone Indians they met. Sacagawea was pregnant, and she gave birth to a son, Jean Baptiste, on February 11, 1805.

It was a bitingly cold winter at Fort Mandan, with temperatures reaching minus 40 degrees Fahrenheit (minus 40 degrees Celsius.) But by late March the ice began to break up on the Missouri River. On April 7 the group sent its biggest boat back to St. Louis with the journals, reports, and samples the men had recorded.

The remaining group consisted of 33 people, including Charbonneau, Sacagawea, and their baby. This began the most exciting and dangerous part of the group's journey. They were heading for the massive Rocky Mountains and intended to cross the great spine of the continent—the Continental Divide. No white people had ever traveled this far west. As William Clark wrote to his brother, "The country before me is extensive and unexplored."

The group made its way up the Missouri River in dugout canoes. The land they traveled through was unlike anything any of them had ever seen. The river flowed through canyons with towering cliffs on either side. On June 13, while scouting ahead of the rest of the group, Lewis and Clark came across the Great Falls of the Missouri River in Montana. It was an incredible sight. But it took the explorers about a month to carry their canoes and supplies around the falls so they could continue up the river.

Soon after passing the falls, the group met some Shoshone Indians. With Sacagawea acting as translator, they traded for some horses to get them over the mountains. The Indians also described the land they were heading into so that Lewis and Clark's party could be better prepared. Even so, the journey ahead was a great challenge.

TACKLING THE MOUNTAINS

The travelers trudged up the mountains through August. As the weeks passed and they reached the higher elevations, the weather began to cool significantly. Water left out overnight had ice on its surface by morning. Though the horses they rode were strong and agile, the landscape was getting rockier and steeper. Near the end of the month, Clark wrote in his journal that they were passing "over rocky hillsides where our horses were in perpetual danger of slipping to their certain destruction, up and down steep hills where several horses fell, some turned over, and others slipped down steep hillsides, one horse crippled and two gave out." Their food supply was also running low.

By mid-September the crew was cold, miserable, and starving. Though the Shoshone Indians had given them advice and provided a guide, the explorers were hacking through very difficult land. They had little luck hunting, and on September 14, Clark wrote that they had to kill one of their colts for food. Water was hard to find, so they melted snow, which was plentiful. On September 16, they killed another colt to eat. The next day they killed another. They traveled only 10 miles (16 km) that day, as the thick snow and rough, rocky terrain made travel difficult. The horses continued to fall, often hurting themselves or damaging the gear they carried. At one point the explorers became so hungry they even considered eating their candles.

Finally, the explorers got through the mountains, after which they met some Nez Perce Indians who fed them fish and roots. After being hungry for so long, their bodies weren't ready for a big meal. Many of them ate too much and got sick. But once they recovered, the Nez Perce helped them make new canoes. The Indians also explained how to travel down the Columbia River to the Pacific Ocean.

Although traveling on the river was sometimes rough, the most difficult part of their journey was behind them. Lewis and Clark completed the trip to the Pacific coast, which was beyond the Louisiana Territory. The team returned in 1806. The group had traveled thousands of miles and survived several dangers along the way. Amazingly, only one man died from an infection he contracted early in the journey. Lewis and Clark's expedition was extremely successful, and the knowledge it gained would help thousands of explorers and pioneers in the coming years.

Statue honoring Sacagawea and her son, Jean-Baptiste, in Portland, Oregon

DID YOU KNOW?

Sacagawea is famous for being the only woman on Lewis and Clark's expedition. Her work as a translator with Indian tribes was vital for the success of the mission. Her knowledge of the land helped her guide the explorers to find a route to the Pacific Ocean. Several statues and memorials across the United States honor her memory. In 2000 the U.S. Mint created a one-dollar coin to honor Sacagawea's achievements.

OUTLASTING DEATH IN THE BLUE MOUNTAINS
MARIE DORION

It was 1814, in the middle of a cold, snowy winter in the Blue Mountains. Marie Dorion was desperate. She had just traveled nearly 200 miles (322 km) alone with her two young sons and two horses. But she wasn't traveling for fun or to seek a new home. She was fleeing a group of Bannock Indians who had earlier attacked and killed her husband and the other men at the Pacific Fur Company outpost. Marie didn't know exactly where she was heading. She just knew she had to get her family to safety.

After crossing the dangerous Snake River and other obstacles, Marie realized she had few options. One of her horses collapsed and died. Her other horse had little strength left, and neither did Marie. Should she try to press on to see if she could find help? Or should she try to find shelter where she was and stay there for the winter?

Marie Dorion was no stranger to dangerous and difficult situations. Born in the 1780s, she was of Iowa Indian and French-Canadian descent. In 1804 she became the common-law wife of Pierre Dorion, which meant they weren't legally married. Pierre's mother was Sioux Indian and his father was French-Canadian. Pierre and Marie lived in what is now Yankton, South Dakota. Their first son, Jean Baptiste, was born in 1806. A few years later they had another son, Paul. The family moved to St. Louis in 1810.

Fort Astoria acted as a major fur-trading post for the Pacific Fur Company. It was located on the Columbia River in present-day Oregon.

While in St. Louis, the Pacific Fur Company recruited Pierre for an expedition to Oregon. Pierre was valuable to the group because of his experience and knowledge of the backcountry along the Missouri River. He also spoke several Indian languages. But he told the fur company that he wouldn't take the job without his wife and sons. The company didn't want the bother of having a woman and children tagging along. But they needed Pierre's skills, so they agreed.

HOME ON THE RANGE

The expedition to Oregon began in the spring of 1811. The journey was grueling. The farther the group traveled, the scarcer the food grew. The horses grew weak and faint. By the end of the journey, the explorers would have to slaughter and eat several of them. The expedition members trudged through rivers and over mountains. When they reached the raging Snake River in Idaho, they built wooden rafts to try to float to their destination. But their rafts were no match for the river's rapids. Two men drowned, and the survivors trudged along on foot.

The westward travel was hard on everyone. But it was especially hard on Marie, who was pregnant with her third child. One day in late December, Marie went into labor. Pierre told the rest of the group to go on ahead. Marie gave birth to her third son in the wilderness. The very next day, she and her family set off on horseback and caught up with the rest of the group. Unfortunately, the new baby died a few weeks later.

When the group reached what is now Caldwell, Idaho, they built a permanent camp. Marie and Pierre made a home for themselves and their children at this main post. While Marie cared for their home and children, Pierre and the other men went out on short trips to trap animals for their furs.

A WARNING

In January 1814, Pierre was out trapping with three partners. They set up a temporary camp about three days' journey away from the main post. One afternoon, a scout rode up to the main post and warned Marie that Bannock Indians were attacking nearby camps. The Bannock were angry that white people were living and trapping on their lands. Marie knew her husband could be killed if she didn't warn him about the attackers.

She bundled up her two young sons and set out on horseback. For three days she rode through rain and mud. But as she neared the spot where her husband's small group had set up camp, she came across one of Pierre's partners. He was weak and badly wounded. He told her that the Bannock had attacked them and killed Pierre and the other two trappers.

Marie knew she had to act fast, both to save herself and her sons, and also to warn others back at the main post. She slung the wounded man over one of the horses and headed back to the post. But the man's injuries were severe, and he died along the way. Marie rode on, hoping to make it to safety.

However, when she arrived at the post, she didn't find safety. She instead found an awful scene. The post had been attacked, and everyone there had been killed. Marie was sure she would face the same fate if the attackers found her. She grabbed her two sons, collected what food she could, and fled westward with two horses.

The Snake River runs through the rugged Blue Mountains in northeastern Oregon.

That's how Marie found herself alone with her two sons and one sick horse in the depth of winter in the Blue Mountains. She thought about going on to try to reach help. But she had no idea if there were even friendly settlements on the other side of the mountains. She also didn't know if she or her boys could make the trip in the winter weather.

WINTER ORDEAL

Marie decided to stay for the winter. Fortunately, she had excellent survival skills. She killed her remaining horse and smoked the meat so it would last longer. From the horsehide she built a shelter with branches and grass. She used horsehair to make small traps to catch mice and squirrels. For the next 53 days, she kept her sons alive in the small shelter. They lived on the horsemeat, any mice or squirrels she could catch, and frozen berries.

In March the snow began to melt, and Marie and her boys resumed their journey on foot. But after just two days, a fierce spring blizzard hit. The entire landscape was covered in deep snow as far as she could see. Staring at the bright white snow caused Marie to lose her vision for several days. The family camped for three days until she could see again and then resumed their trek through the wilderness. Finally, 15 days after leaving their winter shelter, Marie and her sons reached the plains on the other side of the Blue Mountains.

Marie was out of food and nearly exhausted. But she spotted a pillar of smoke on the horizon. People! She didn't know if they were friendly or hostile. But they were her only hope. Marie was too weak to walk in the direction of the smoke. She hid the boys near a large rock and crawled toward the smoke. She was overjoyed when she reached a village of Walla Walla Indians who took her in and sent a group out to rescue her sons.

Once Marie regained her strength, she remained in the Oregon area. She married twice more and had three more children. Marie died in 1850 near present-day Salem, Oregon.

IN HONOR OF
MADAME MARIE DORION
COURAGEOUS PIONEER
DEVOTED IOWAY MOTHER
EARLY OREGON SETTLER

AT THIS HER FINAL RESTING PLACE
SEPTEMBER 6, 1850

PLACED BY CHAMPOEG CHAPTER
DAUGHTERS OF THE AMERICAN REVOLUTION
MAY 10, 2014

DID YOU KNOW?

Today, Madame Dorion Memorial Park in the foothills of the
Blue Mountains in Washington memorializes Marie Dorion.
A plaque notes the spot where she likely gave birth to her
baby boy. In 2014 an engraved stone monument honoring
Marie's memory was placed at her grave in Oregon.

GLOSSARY

banish—to send away forever

Continental Divide—the stretch of high ground formed by the crests of the Rocky Mountains. Rivers on the east flow to the Atlantic and rivers on the west flow to the Pacific.

crevasse—a deep, wide crack in a glacier or ice sheet

elevation—the height of the land above sea level

expedition—a journey made for a specific purpose

frontier—the far edge beyond a settled area, where few people live

frontiersman—a person who is skilled at living outside settled lands

gangrene—a condition that occurs when body tissues become severely infected and begin to decay

hallucinate—to see things that aren't really there

malnutrition—a condition caused by a lack of healthy food

oxbow—a U-shaped bend in a river; also a U-shaped harness used to attach oxen to a wagon to pull it

pioneer—someone who explores or settles in a new land

rations—limited amounts or shares, especially of food

rebellion—a fight or struggle against those in charge when people feel they are being treated unfairly

terrain—the surface of the land

territory—an area of land that is controlled by a country

READ MORE

Lassieur, Allison. *Westward Expansion: An Interactive History Adventure*. North Mankato, MN: Capstone Press, 2016.

Rajczak Nelson, Kristen. *The Donner Party*. New York: Gareth Stevens Publishing, 2016.

Russo, Kristin J. *Viewpoints on the Oregon Trail and Westward Expansion*. Ann Arbor, MI: Cherry Lake Publishing, 2019.

INTERNET SITES

America Heads West
https://kids.nationalgeographic.com/explore/history/lewis-and-clark/

Oregon Trail
https://www.history.com/topics/westward-expansion/oregon-trail

Westward Expansion: Daily Life on the Frontier
https://www.ducksters.com/history/westward_expansion/daily_life_on_the_frontier.php

SOURCE NOTES

p. 17, "Although I had lost my rifle…," "Quest for Revenge." An Unforgettable Man: Hugh Glass. http://hughglass.org/quest-for-revenge/, Accessed August 14, 2019.

p. 35, "We ate his head and feet…" Ethan Rarick. *Desperate Passage: The Donner Party's Perilous Journey West.* New York: Oxford University Press, 2008, page 158.

p. 35, "Are you men from California…" Ibid, page 170.

p. 42, "Mr. Walker was a man well calculated…" Bil Gilbert. *Westering Man: The Life of Joseph Walker.* New York: Atheneum, 1983, page 123.

p. 43, "in the direction of a mountain, …" Scott Stine. *A Way Across the Mountain: Joseph Walker's 1833 Trans-Sierran Passage and Myth of Yosemite's Discovery.* Norman: University of Oklahoma Press, 2015, page 91.

p. 43, "awfully sublime." Gilbert, 134.

p. 44, "stupid and stiff." Ibid, 134.

p. 44, "nothing to eat worth mentioning." Stine, 136.

p. 44, "We camped this night on the south side…" Ibid, 136.

p. 45, "This gave our men fresh courage…" Gilbert, 135.

p. 51, "The country before me is extensive and unexplored." James J. Holmberg. *Into the Wilderness: The Lewis and Clark Expedition.* Lexington: The University Press of Kentucky, 2003, page 30.

p. 52, "over rocky hillsides where our horses were in perpetual danger…" Meriwether Lewis and William Clark. *The Journals of Lewis and Clark*, abridged by Anthony Brandt. Washington, DC: National Geographic Society, 2002.

BIBLIOGRAPHY

An Unforgettable Man: Hugh Glass. http://hughglass.org/. Accessed August 13, 2019.

Brown, Daniel James. *The Indifferent Stars Above: The Harrowing Saga of a Donner Party Bride.* New York: William Morrow, 2009.

Dixon, Kelly J., Shannon A. Novak, Gwen Robbins, Julie M. Schablitsky, G. Richard Scott, and Guy L. Tasa. "'Men, Women, and Children Starving': Archaeology of the Donner Family Camp," *American Antiquity,* 75(3), 2010, 627–656.

Fowler, William Worthington. *Woman on the American Frontier.* New York: Source Book Press, 1970, c1876.

French, Brett. "Hugh Glass, Mountain Man: 'Revenant' Tale Intertwines with Montana History," *The Montana Standard.* January 17, 2016.

Gilbert, Bil. *Westering Man.* New York: Atheneum, 1983.

History.com: Lewis and Clark. https://www.history.com/topics/westward-expansion/lewis-and-clark. Accessed August 13, 2019.

History of American Women: Marie Dorion. http://www.womenhistoryblog.com/2012/08/marie-dorion.html. Accessed August 12, 2019.

Holmberg, James J. *Into the Wilderness: The Lewis and Clark Expedition.* Lexington: The University Press of Kentucky, 2003.

Johnson, Kristin. New Light on the Donner Party. https://user.xmission.com/~octa/DonnerParty/index.html. Accessed August 12, 2019.

Lewis, Meriwether, and William Clark. *The Journals of Lewis and Clark.* Abridged by Anthony Brandt. Washington, DC: National Geographic Society, 2002.

Lyons, Chuck. "Stranded in the Rockies." *Wild West* magazine, April 2018.

Rarick, Ethan. *Desperate Passage: The Donner Party's Perilous Journey West.* New York: Oxford University Press, 2008.

Shirley, Gayle C. *More than Petticoats: Remarkable Oregon Women.* Helena, MT: TwoDot, 1998.

Stine, Scott. *A Way Across the Mountain: Joseph Walker's 1833 Trans-Sierran Passage and the Myth of Yosemite's Discovery.* Norman: University of Oklahoma Press, 2015.

Ruland-Thorne, Kate. Westering Walker. https://www.historynet.com/westering-walker.htm. Accessed September 9, 2019.

INDEX

ABOUT THE AUTHOR

Eric Braun is the author of dozens of books for kids and teens on many topics including sports, the deep state, overcoming mistakes, and fractured fairy tales. He lives in Minneapolis with his wife, two sons, and a dog named Willis.